W9-BIX-864

A New Brother or Sister

Charlotte Guillain

Heinemann Library
Chicago, Illinois

www.heinemannraintree.com

Visit our website to find out more information about Heinemann-Raintree books.

To order:

☎ Phone 888-454-2279

🖥 Visit www.heinemannraintree.com to browse our catalog and order online.

© 2011 Heinemann Library
an imprint of Capstone Global Library, LLC
Chicago, Illinois

All rights reserved. No part of this publication may be reproduced or transmitted in any form or by any means, electronic or mechanical, including photocopying, recording, taping, or any information storage and retrieval system, without permission in writing from the publisher.

Edited by Dan Nunn, Rebecca Rissman, and Sian Smith
Designed by Joanna Hinton-Malivoire
Picture research by Elizabeth Alexander
Originated by Capstone Global Library Ltd
Printed and bound in the United States of America, North Mankato, MN.

15 14 13 12 11
10 9 8 7 6 5 4 3 2

Library of Congress Cataloging-in-Publication Data
Guillain, Charlotte.
  A new brother or sister / Charlotte Guillain.
    p. cm.—(Growing up)
  Includes bibliographical references and index.
  ISBN 978-1-4329-4803-0 (hc)—ISBN 978-1-4329-4813-9 (pb) 1. Infants—Juvenile literature. 2. Brothers and sisters—Juvenile literature. I. Title.
  HQ774.G85 2011
  306.875'3—dc22   2010024197

062011
006151RP

Acknowledgments

We would like to thank the following for permission to reproduce photographs: Alamy pp. 8 (© Glow Wellness RM 97), 12, 23 glossary nappy (© Bubbles Photolibrary), 18 (© Picture Press); © Capstone Publishers pp. 17, 19 (Karon Dubke); Corbis p. 11 (© David P. Hall); Getty Images pp. 4, 23 glossary pregnant (Lori Adamski Peek/Workbook Stock), 5 (Michael Wildsmith/Taxi), 20 (Tony Anderson/Taxi); iStockphoto pp. 10 (© zhang bo), 14 (© jo unruh), 22 bottom middle (© Jenny Swanson); Photolibrary pp. 6, 23 glossary hospital (Corbis), 7 (Image Source), 9, 23 glossary incubator (Upitis Alvis/Imagestate), 16 (Nicole Hill/Rubberball), 21, glossary jealous (Picture Partners/age footstock); Shutterstock pp. 13 (© Reynardt), 15 (© Monkey Business Images), 22 top left (© jcpjr), 22 top middle (© Lim Yong Hian), 22 top right (© Myotis), 22 bottom left (© Stephen Coburn), 22 bottom right (© Margo Harrison).

Front cover photograph of a girl holding a baby reproduced with permission of Photolibrary (Clarissa Leahy). Back cover photographs of baby clothes reproduced with permission of © Capstone Publishers (Karon Dubke), and a bath reproduced with permission of iStockphoto (© jo unruh).

Every effort has been made to contact copyright holders of material reproduced in this book. Any omissions will be rectified in subsequent printings if notice is given to the publisher.

Disclaimer

All the Internet addresses (URLs) given in this book were valid at the time of going to press. However, due to the dynamic nature of the Internet, some addresses may have changed or ceased to exist since publication. While the author and publisher regret any inconvenience this may cause readers, no responsibility for any such changes can be accepted by either the author or the publisher.

Contents

Some words are shown in bold, **like this**.
You can find them in the glossary on page 23.

What Happens Before a New Baby Arrives?

When your family is expecting a new baby, your mom will be **pregnant**.

Her stomach will get bigger and she may be more tired than normal.

Your family will need to get ready for the new baby.

They will find your old baby things and maybe buy some new things.

What Happens When the Baby Is Born?

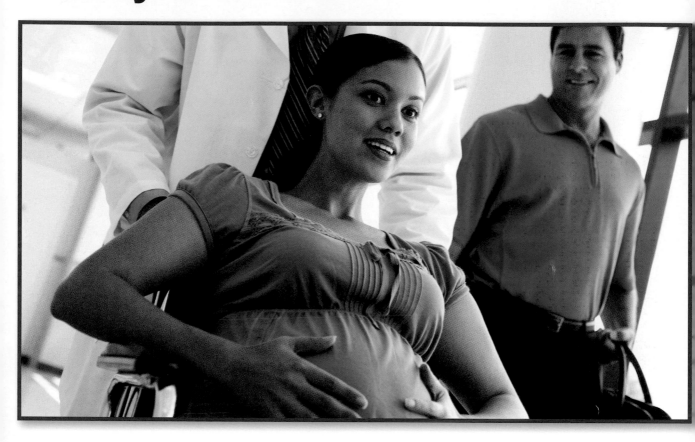

Your mom will probably go to the **hospital** to have the baby.

She may have to leave for the hospital quite suddenly or quickly.

You might go to stay with relatives or friends while your mom is in the hospital.

You might miss your mom, but there is no need to feel scared or worried.

When Will I Meet My New Brother or Sister?

You might visit your mom and the baby in the **hospital**.

Or you might meet your brother or sister when your mom brings him or her home.

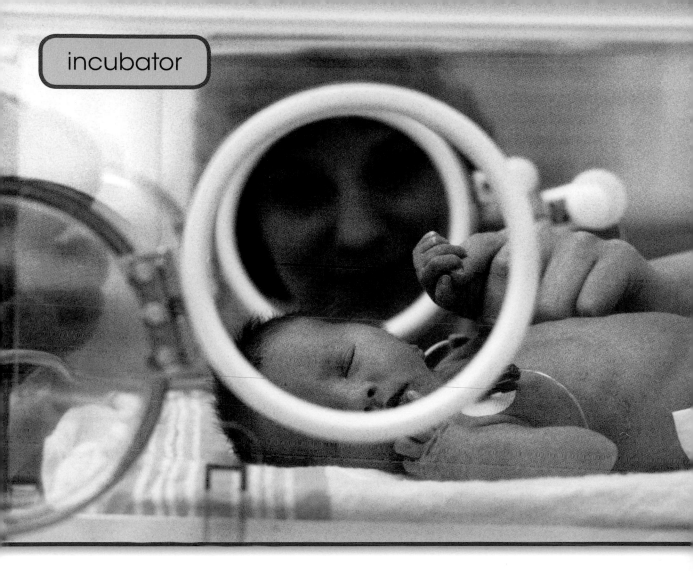

incubator

Some babies have to stay in the hospital for a while so that the doctors can look after them.

Some babies stay in an **incubator** until they are strong enough to go home.

What Are New Babies Like?

New babies spend a lot of time sleeping.

They cannot sit up or stand until they are much older.

New babies cry and need your mom or dad a lot of the time.

You need to be very gentle with a new brother or sister.

What Do New Babies Need?

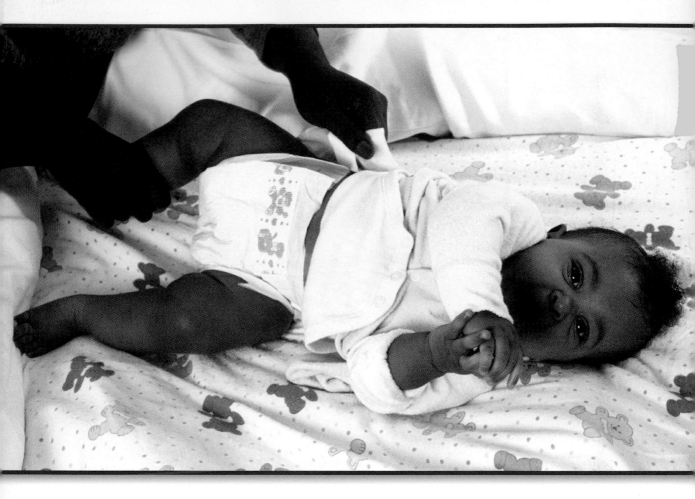

Babies need **diapers** because they cannot use the bathroom yet.

They also need a special car seat to keep them safe in the car.

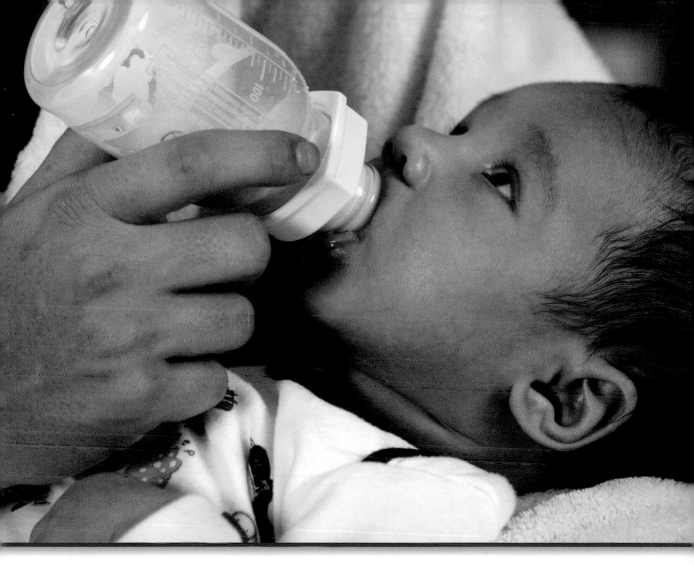

New babies can drink milk many times during the day and night.

They also need lots of sleep in the daytime and at night.

Why Does the Baby Need My Parents?

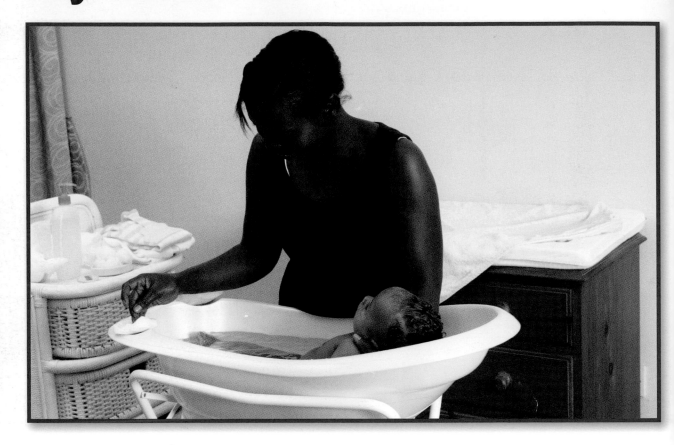

Your mom or dad has to feed, wash, and change the baby many times a day.

They also need to cuddle the baby when he or she cries.

Your mom and dad will be sorry that they cannot spend more time with you.

You can try to do things together when the baby sleeps.

Can I Help Take Care of the New Baby?

Your mom or dad might not want you to pick up the baby.

If the baby is crying, you could make him or her laugh by talking or singing.

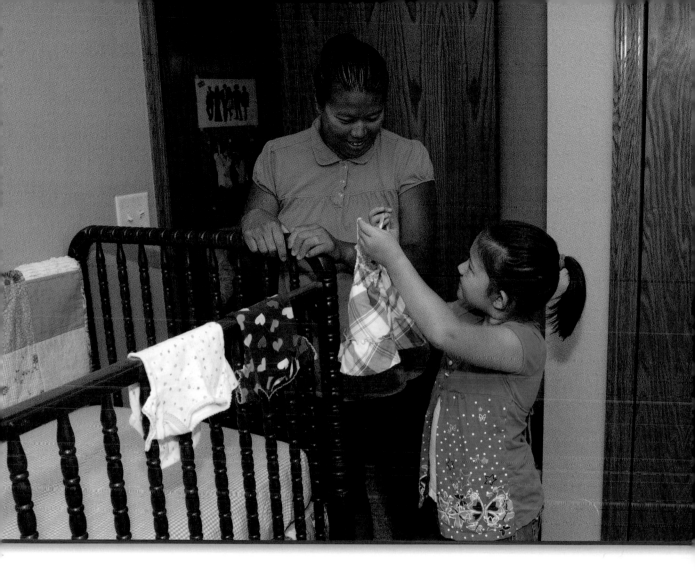

You can bring things that your mom or dad needs when they feed or change the baby.

You might be able to help choose what the baby is going to wear.

Can the Baby Play with Me?

New babies will not be able to play with you until they are older.

When they are little, you can show babies toys and books.

When they start crawling, they may want to play with your toys.

You could put your special things away on a shelf.

How Does the Baby Make My Family Feel?

Your parents will feel very happy, but they will also be very tired.

They might get upset more than usual because they are so tired.

You might feel **jealous** of the baby for taking up so much of your parents' time.

You might feel excited and proud to have a new brother or sister.

Baby Equipment

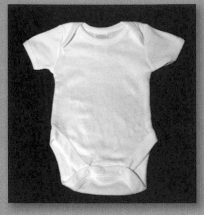
clothes

bottle

diaper

crib

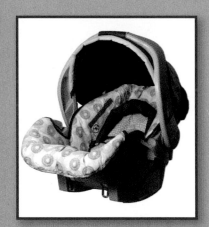
car seat

high chair

Picture Glossary

 **diaper** towel or special underpants worn by babies because they cannot use the bathroom

 **hospital** place where sick people are made better and where many women have babies

 **incubator** place that keeps new babies at the right temperature

 **jealous** when you feel bad because you want something somebody else has

 **pregnant** expecting a baby

Find Out More

Books

Andreae, Giles, and Vanessa Cabban. *There's a House Inside My Mommy*. Morton Grove, Il.: Albert Whitman, 2002.

Anholt, Catherine, and Laurence Anholt. *Sophie and the New Baby*. Morton Grove, Il.: Albert Whitman, 2000.

Civardi, Anna, and Stephen Cartwright. *The New Baby*. Tulsa, Okla.: EDC, 2005.

Murloff, Heidi Eisenberg. *What to Expect When Mommy's Having a Baby*. New York: HarperFestival, 2000.

Websites

Find out more about welcoming a new baby into the family at:
http://kidshealth.org/kid/feeling/home_family/new_baby.html

Index

306.875 G   ICCRX
Guillain, Charlotte.
A new brother or sister /
CENTRAL LIBRARY
10/11

Friends of the
Houston Public Library